LIVING

AS AN

OVERCOMER

WORKBOOK

TONY EVANS

HARVEST HOUSE PUBLISHERS
EUGENE. OREGON

Cover design by Studio Gearbox

Cover images © White_Engine, FMStox / Shutterstock

Interior design by KUHN Design Group

For bulk, special sales, or ministry purchases, please call 1-800-547-8979. Email: Customerservice@hhpbooks.com

Living as an Overcomer Workbook
Copyright © 2023 by Tony Evans
Published by Harvest House Publishers
Eugene, Oregon 97408
www.harvesthousepublishers.com

ISBN 978-0-7369-8815-5 (pbk)
ISBN 978-0-7369-8816-2 (eBook)

Printed in the United States of America

23 24 25 26 27 28 29 30 31 / BP / 10 9 8 7 6 5 4 3 2 1

CONTENTS

ACKNOWLEDGMENTS

I want to thank my friends at Harvest House Publishers for their long-standing partnership in bringing my thoughts, study, and words to print. I particularly want to thank Bob Hawkins for his friendship over the years as well as for his pursuit of excellence in leading his company. I also want to publicly thank Kim Moore and Jean Bloom for their help in the editorial process.

Working with the team at RightNow Media is always a pleasure, and they bring great professionalism and talent to what they do as well as a love for our Lord. Thank you, Phil Warner, for leading your group so well, and many thanks to the entire team that filmed and edited this study. In addition, my appreciation goes to Heather Hair for her skills and insights in collaboration on this Bible study content and assistance with the video production.

MAKING THE MOST
OF THIS WORKBOOK

This *Living as an Overcomer Workbook* is designed to help you and your group combine the video teaching you'll view, the Bible study you'll take on, and the experience you'll share into a dynamic growth encounter.

Each of the eight sessions based on the *Living as an Overcomer* book by Tony Evans includes the following sections, all of which will help you and your group make the most of both your community and personal experiences during this study. Don't hesitate to make notes in the space provided between suggestions and questions or in the margins.

COMMIT TO MEMORY

This section not only provides the foundational Bible verse or verses for each session but encourages you to memorize Scripture. You may want to review the Scripture in upcoming sessions in advance to begin the process of memorization.

CONSIDER

This section gives you key insights from Tony Evans and the *Living as an Overcomer* book, setting the stage for the rest of the session. But because the book has much more information and many more illustrations than you'll find here, you may want to read or reread the relevant book chapter for each session in this study in advance.

CONNECT

The suggestions and questions here are designed to inspire sharing that will help group members connect—or if you've gathered before, connect even better. We all come to small group settings with our own history, background, personality, passions, and purpose, and the events of our lives coupled with who we are as people have shaped both our mindsets and approaches to life and to others. Our willingness to share our experiences can help encourage other group members to share theirs, and everyone can grow as a result. God uses the good, the bad, and the ugly to bring about His good in our lives when we love Him and are living as called people according to His purpose.

This Connect time should always open with prayer, inviting God's Spirit to manifest Himself fully in your midst, soften your hearts and ears to His Word, and guard your lips, seasoning each person's speech as with salt. Try to save prayer requests and praise for answered prayer for the end of the session since this time is specifically designed to connect with one another and God.

CAPTURE

Next you'll watch Tony's video teaching for the session.

CONCENTRATE

Most of these suggestions and questions are designed to encourage discussion following the video as everyone recalls what they just viewed. Others might help you connect the teaching to your personal experiences or emotions. This section also features Scripture to promote spiritual growth through the reading and study of God's Word.

CONVERGE

This section is designed to help you and the group explore how your daily lives and the wisdom you've gained in this study can converge—in other words, to help you determine how you can apply what you've learned in this session. Extra space is provided for personal notes and proposed action steps you can refer to in the coming days.

CONCLUDE

To close the session, first worship the Lord together in any way meaningful to the group, such as singing a song. Then before a final prayer, share any prayer requests or praise for answered prayer.

CONTINUE

This last section—divided into five parts—is designed to help you dig deeper throughout the following days on your own, keeping the session's content and principles fresh in your mind and encouraging you to put what you've learned and purposed into practice.

FOR LEADERS AND FACILITATORS

Ensure that each group member has their own workbook. This will allow everyone to not only make personal notes during the session but to use the Continue section.

- Consider logistics in the setting for your gathering so no one in the group will be distracted by discomfort or miss anything. Will everyone have a comfortable seat? Is the lighting adequate? Will they all be able to clearly see the video? Is the audio set at a good level? You might also want to have some extra pens or pencils handy.

- Ahead of time or with the group at the first session, decide if someone will read the Consider section aloud as other members follow along or if each member should read it in advance.

- To prepare personal responses that could encourage the flow of discussion, review the suggestions and questions throughout each session. You may also want to flag discussion prompters that seem most significant for your group in case you start running short of time and need to move on.

WELCOME!

We all need to overcome something—a circumstance, an emotion, a habit, or a situation that holds us back. But guess what? Not only does God want you to overcome life's challenges, but He's provided the way for you to do it. That's why I've chosen to teach on the seven churches in the book of Revelation and develop this eight-session video curriculum.

One at a time, we'll study these seven churches and the important message Jesus sent to each of them through an angel and the apostle John. Then we'll allow the principles we learn to reveal how we can live as overcomers both within the church and in the world around us. You are to live as a victor, not a victim, and so I aim to equip you with all you need to experience that reality. Toward that end, you'll not only go through the written material in this workbook but view the videos I filmed in a city appropriate for this study—Las Vegas!

This curriculum is designed to integrate learning and community, and the seven churches in Revelation will be studied within the context of community. We are all meant to do life with other people, and in a group setting, we can build community as we learn, socialize, pray, worship, and grow together. But if you choose to go through this curriculum alone, the study can still help you learn and reflect on all that God is teaching you.

Either way, my prayer is that you'll experience God in a fresh way, finding all you need to overcome anything and everything that's holding you back. So get ready for growth because the principles for and the keys to overcoming will challenge, convict, and mature you. What's more, they will reward you as you learn to overcome whatever it is you face.

My prayer is that by the time you've completed this study, you will have laid claim to all God has in store for you. Let nothing hinder you from living out your God-ordained purpose with both passion and freedom.

For His kingdom,
Tony Evans

THE KEY TO OVERCOMING

COMMIT TO MEMORY

Whatever is born of God overcomes the world; and this is the victory that has overcome the world—our faith. Who is the one who overcomes the world, but he who believes that Jesus is the Son of God? (1 John 5:4-5).

CONSIDER

Before we move into a time of connecting, take in these key insights gleaned from Tony Evans and the *Living as an Overcomer* book. They set the stage for the rest of the session.

No matter where you live or where you come from, you've most likely seen the Nike swoosh logo. *Nike* is a Greek word that means "to overcome." It makes sense that a shoe company would be named with a word that means overcoming. After all, sports and athletics are all about overcoming. Whether it's overcoming your opponent by scoring more points or overcoming your own fears and limitations through pushing yourself, athletics are built around this concept. Overcoming appeals to all of us, because like it or not, we all face challenges in life that put us in a position of either accepting defeat or needing to overcome.

That could be why Jesus repeatedly used the term *overcome* when he instructed John to communicate His messages to the seven churches in the book of Revelation. They were all about what kept the believers in those days stuck. They needed to know what and how to overcome in order to live with full commitment to Christ. Whether the challenge of temptation, the challenge of personal sin, or the challenge of aligning their spiritual priorities with God's, these churches had a lot to overcome.

I think you'll see that these churches' experiences were not too far removed from where Christians are in the world today. Thousands of years have passed, but the problems and distractions that drew these people away from God are similar to the problems and distractions we struggle with now. Our focus over these eight sessions, then, will be on walking into the full realization and experience of spiritual freedom through this process of learning how to overcome.

You can find many mentions of the number seven in the Bible, and in Revelation, it comes up regularly. Seven is the number of completeness and fullness. It often means something has reached full expression. It can also signify perfection. And in Jesus' messages to these seven churches, we can infer that He wants them all to be complete, fulfilled, and not lacking. Why? Because He's given a series of unique messages cumulatively arriving at the number seven as though to say if they collectively overcome in these seven areas, they will overcome completely and perfectly.

Seven times Christ says the same exact thing when He addresses the churches in Revelation: "He who has an ear, let him hear." Even though they all have their own uniqueness, problems, pressures, and burdens—as do we—the message to each church boils down to the same solution: Jesus says the person who has an external ear needs to hear the internal message from the Spirit of God.

We've all talked to people who heard our words but didn't get our message, so we understand when Jesus suggests it's possible to have an ear and not hear, that it's possible to still not get the truth. He's saying that whoever has the capacity to receive the data ought to take heed to it, because the hearing with the ear has as its goal the heeding of the truth.

I'm sure you've heard the civil rights song "We Shall Overcome," a call to living victoriously over adverse injustices. Overcoming is not a small matter; it's a serious one.

When Jesus speaks of overcoming, He's not giving a motivational speech; He's giving people a kingdom perspective. A worldview that involves both a state and a standing. We know it's a state, because in 1 John 5, John says those who believe in Christ have overcome the world. They are within a stated position in

Jesus Christ. In other words, since Christ has overcome and we are His followers, we're already overcomers by our position in Him.

But God wants our state of being to be more than that. He wants our position to become our practice. That's why we who are believers in Christ can overcome the world (1 John 5:5). We are to do more than simply live in Christ's position of overcoming. We, too, are overcomers in our everyday lives.

Let me illustrate this with marriage. If a couple is married, they're legally married whether or not they're happily married. A legal status exists for all married couples. But there's also a relational practice available to every couple, to either take advantage of or neglect. Legal status in marriage does not automatically mean a happy marriage.

Every believer has been positioned as an overcomer because of their status with the One who has overcome, Jesus Christ. But it's up to every Christian to individually turn that position into a practice. It's up to you to make what is legal in heaven, literal in history. Doing so is the process we call "overcoming."

Please notice one more thing that has a major impact. Jesus says to hear what the Spirit of God says to the church, which is made up of individual people. But His address is to the individual person who has an ear. In other words, there's one message for the whole congregation, but you must decide whether you will individually pay attention to it and allow the Spirit to speak to you directly. Going to church—or even to a small group—won't send the truth of God deep within your spirit. Only when you choose to hear and apply His truth will the fruit of it—the ability to overcome—be made manifest in your life.

Excerpted from chapter 1, *Living as an Overcomer*

CONNECT

After praying together, respond to these suggestions or questions, remembering that sharing is part of connecting with others.

1. What motivated you to participate in a small group like this one?

2. What do you hope to get out of this study and group experience?

3. How do you think you can best contribute to the overall health of this group and your time together?

CAPTURE

Settle back and watch Tony's video teaching, taking in what he's been led to share for this session. The next section will help you unpack what you hear.

CONCENTRATE

The following questions, suggestions, and Scripture passages are designed to guide your discussion in response to Tony's teaching in the video.

1. Read each of these verses: Revelation 2:7, 11, 17, 26; 3:5, 12, 21. What is the common word or phrase repeated in each one?

2. According to our Commit to Memory Scripture this week—1 John 5:4-5—who has the ability to overcome the world?

3. What is the victory that gives us the ability to overcome?

4. Tony often defines faith as acting like God is telling the truth. In what ways does faith involve more than our feelings?

5. Based on the video teaching, what is the key to overcoming? Refer to John 16:33 if you need help in answering this question.

CONVERGE

Explore how what you've learned in this session can converge with your daily life—in other words, how you can apply it. As you discuss the following, jot down personal notes and proposed action steps in the extra space provided.

1. In what situation did you feel you had faith, but then when you needed to act on that faith, you realized you didn't have as much faith as you thought?

2. What role does faith play in overcoming? Share in what area of your life you desire greater faith. What steps can you take to pursue it?

3. Read Revelation 21:7. This verse speaks of a special, uniquely intimate relationship between a believer and God. Describe how you know when you're experiencing a uniquely intimate relationship with God. Can you share a personal example of His powerful presence in your life?

4. Revelation 1:12-20 talks about a warrior Jesus who doesn't necessarily resemble the meek and mild Jesus we see in paintings and drawings. What image of Jesus do you perceive when you think of Him? Is it the meek and mild Jesus? Or the Jesus described in this passage in Revelation? In what ways does Jesus embody all of these aspects?

5. How does knowing these characteristics of Jesus revealed in Revelation 1:12-20 strengthen your faith and empower your thoughts regarding your own overcoming?

CONCLUDE

To close the session, first worship the Lord together in any way meaningful to the group, such as singing a song. Then before a final prayer, share any prayer requests or praise for answered prayer.

CONTINUE

This last section is for you to use on your own over the next week, proceeding through the five opportunities for reflection as you wish—perhaps one per day. Before you work through the Scripture and questions, ask the Lord to open your ears to truly hear His truth and for His help in applying it in your life. Then record what He reveals to you in the extra space provided.

1. Read John 16:33: "These things I have spoken to you, so that in Me you may have peace. In the world you have tribulation, but take courage; I have overcome the world."

   Reflect
   What seems to steal your peace? Why do you think that happens?

   How can you place greater faith in Christ in order to tap into the peace He has for you?

   Why are we to "take courage"? Based on what truth?

2. Read Colossians 2:15: "When He had disarmed the rulers and authorities, He made a public display of them, having triumphed over them through Him."

Reflect

In what specific situation do you need God's power this week?

Jesus triumphed over the enemy and disarmed them. How can this truth strengthen you to live as an overcomer?

In what ways are you giving Satan more authority than he rightfully has? How can you change that? Will you commit to making it a priority to change your mindset and align it with God's Word?

3. Read Revelation 1:14: "His head and His hair were white like white wool, like snow; and His eyes were like a flame of fire."

Reflect

Most of us think of Jesus as a meek and mild Savior like we saw in Bible story books or art pieces growing up. Jesus is a meek and mild Savior in many ways. But Revelation 1:14 lets us in on His warrior side. Is this a side of Jesus unfamiliar to you? How do you feel about this characteristic?

In what ways does knowing Jesus and His power in this way comfort you?

How can a comprehension of these characteristics of Christ assist you in overcoming?

4. Read Revelation 1:6: "He has made us to be a kingdom, priests to His God and Father—to Him be the glory and the dominion forever and ever. Amen."

Reflect

What does it mean to be a kingdom and priests to God?

Are you fully living out this purpose and appointment in your life? If so, how so? If not, what's holding you back?

In what ways can you adjust your thoughts, mindsets, and choices to better reflect the high calling you've been given in Revelation 1:6?

5. Review 1 John 5:4-5: "Whatever is born of God overcomes the world; and this is the victory that has overcome the world—our faith. Who is the one who overcomes the world, but he who believes that Jesus is the Son of God?"

Reflect

What do you think it means that our faith has overcome the world?

If you're struggling under the circumstances or emotions of life, will increasing your faith help you overcome? How so?

How can you increase your faith? Be as specific as you can.

Why is it important to have faith in Jesus, the Son of God, to live as an overcomer?

PUTTING GOD IN FIRST PLACE

COMMIT TO MEMORY

Remember from where you have fallen, and repent and do the deeds you did at first; or else I am coming to you and will remove your lampstand out of its place—unless you repent (Revelation 2:5).

CONSIDER

Before we move into a time of connecting, take in these key insights gleaned from Tony Evans and the *Living as an Overcomer* book. They set the stage for the rest of the session.

Have you ever entered a hotel room or business and found fruit set out as though for the taking? If you have, maybe you've been tempted to take a piece and eat it. The problem is that a lot of fruit on display like that is plastic. It's not real. The fruit might look like apples, oranges, or pears, but it's merely painted plastic. Something can look the part without reality to back it up.

This can happen to Christians too. Many go to church, carry their Bibles, sing praise songs, and say prayers, but looking and sounding the part of a Christian doesn't mean your heart is in it. The heart is revealed through what a person prioritizes, and priorities show up only when push comes to shove or when choices have to be made. If a believer prioritizes Jesus Christ, they won't need to be nudged or reminded to spend time with Him. Only when we settle with looking the part do we need extra incentives for growing in our relationship with God.

The first church addressed in our study on overcomers is the one in Ephesus. In many ways, you could say that Ephesus Bible Fellowship has a lot going on. They're doing many things right. But there's one thing they aren't doing well at all, and Jesus tells them what it is in Revelation 5:4: "You have left your first love." You can't get any more straightforward than that.

If you and I are to live as overcomers in our daily lives, God must not only be loved by us but be loved *first*. The issue with the church in Ephesus is not that they no longer love God at all; it's that they no longer love Him first. He's no longer their priority.

Did you know God can't do certain things? For example, God cannot sin. His nature is pure, and so if He were to sin, He would be going against His nature, and that He cannot do. Another thing God can't do is come in second place. In fact, throughout Scripture, He rightfully *demands* to be first in our lives. He wants to be first in your affections. He wants to be first in your commitment. He wants to be first in your heart.

That's why through John, Jesus called the Ephesus church out for having removed God from first place in their lives. Even though they'd begun their walk and spiritual life with great fervor and prioritization of God, over time they began to lose interest. They started putting other things ahead of God. Even though they were still doing a number of things really well—such as serving, sacrificing, and remaining steadfast—they had left their first love.

The church in Ephesus had plenty of religious activity. They had plenty of worship services. They had plenty of programs and ministries. But regardless of what they did in the name of God, they had left their first love for Him. He was no longer the primary focal point in their affections.

A lot of us have a good list of what we're doing for God, but how we're deepening our relationship with God is on a very short list. Whenever devotion to a relationship leaves, the relationship is in trouble. God doesn't just want our programming. He wants our passion. He wants the fire.

How many couples have talked about the fire in their relationship disappearing? They've "drifted apart." But for the fire to stay hot in a fireplace, there must be an ongoing, intimate connection between the logs. Once that connection disappears, so does the fire. It doesn't matter if you have a million matches at that point, the fire may light, but it will soon go out. To keep a fire burning, the logs must be intimately connected, because the logs keep each other hot.

This is similar to how many people approach their relationship with God. They seek to be lit with a match, such as by going to church and singing worship songs. But by the time they hit the parking lot, the fire is gone. Their spiritual vitality has disappeared, because what started as a relationship with God has devolved into a ritual. What started as intimacy drifted into activity. They lost their fire. They left their first love.

Jesus Christ didn't sacrifice His life on the cross for religion; He sacrificed His life for a relationship. Thus, when He sees religion replacing a relationship, it burdens Him. It saddens Him. He gave His life to be the primary focus of your devotion.

This is what Jesus is saying to the church in Ephesus and to each one of us who has ears to hear: Duty is never to replace devotion. Rather, devotion is to transform duty into something desirable, done out of a heart of love and generated by a relationship rooted in the priority of intimacy.

Excerpted from chapter 2, *Living as an Overcomer*

CONNECT

After praying together, respond to these suggestions or questions, remembering that sharing is part of connecting with others.

1. Describe the difference between a spiritual relationship with God and a ritual.

2. How does legalism negatively affect someone's relationship with the Lord?

3. Share any history or struggle you've had with legalism. If the Lord has set you free from legalism, describe that process. If you're not yet free from it, consider asking the group to remember you in prayer.

4. Collectively review last week's Commit to Memory verses: "Whatever is born of God overcomes the world; and this is the victory that has overcome the world— our faith. Who is the one who overcomes the world, but he who believes that Jesus is the Son of God?" (1 John 5:4-5). Then share how these verses have opened your eyes and ears to hear God speak to you about the truth they contain.

CAPTURE

Settle back and watch Tony's video teaching, taking in what he's been led to share for this session. The next section will help you unpack what you hear.

CONCENTRATE

The following questions, suggestions, and Scripture passages are designed to guide your discussion in response to Tony's teaching in the video.

1. Read Revelation 2:1-7.

   • What are some of the things the people at the church in Ephesus had done well?

• Are these things easy to do? Or would they be considered challenging?

• From where had the church in Ephesus fallen?

2. What three things did Tony say the church in Ephesus was asked to do?

    1.

    2.

    3.

3. Give a tangible example for each of these three steps Christ called the church in Ephesus to take.

    1.

    2.

    3.

4. Will remembering, repenting, and repeating negate or remove the things the church in Ephesus had previously been doing? Why or why not?

5. In what ways could these three steps enhance what the church was already doing for the Lord?

CONVERGE

Explore how what you've learned in this session can converge with your daily life—in other words, how you can apply it. As you discuss the following, jot down personal notes and proposed actions in the extra space provided.

1. Describe a time when it was obvious that you'd left your first love in your relationship with God. What brought this to your attention, and how did you address it? (It's not necessary to give details too personal as you share.)

2. What role does prioritizing Christ first play in overcoming? Give a tangible example (could be fictional) where the program of religion trumped the relationship. How do you think this makes God feel?

3. Read each of the following verses:

   • Exodus 20:5

   • Exodus 34:14

   • Deuteronomy 4:24

- Deuteronomy 32:16

- Joshua 24:19

- Psalm 79:5

- 2 Corinthians 11:12

Do these verses give you a greater understanding of the heart of God toward you? How so? Will the truth of these verses impact and influence your choices? If so, in what way?

4. What is your understanding of what those who overcome at the church in Ephesus will inherit?

5. Have you ever experienced God in a personal, intimate way that you're willing to share with the group? Or have you witnessed someone with this kind of personal relationship with the Lord?

6. Read Matthew 22:37: "You shall love the Lord your God with all your heart, and with all your soul, and with all your mind." Give a practical example or two of what it means to live out this instruction from Christ in your daily life. (Give time for several people to answer. Their answers can encourage others' walk and open their mind to ways of deepening their relationship with God.)

CONCLUDE

To close the session, first worship the Lord together in any way meaningful to the group, such as singing a song. Then before a final prayer, share any prayer requests or praise for answered prayer.

CONTINUE

This last section is for you to use on your own over the next week, proceeding through the five opportunities for reflection as you wish—perhaps one per day. Before you work through the Scripture and questions, ask the Lord to open your ears to truly hear His truth and for His help in applying it in your life. Then record what He reveals to you in the extra space provided.

1. Read Deuteronomy 6:5: "You shall love the LORD your God with all your heart and with all your soul and with all your might."

   Reflect

   In what areas of your life do you find competition for putting God first? Are you willing to repent of the things you put before God in your life and ask Him to help you put Him in His rightful place?

   What are some practical things you can do (or not do) that will demonstrate this position of loving God with all your heart, soul, and might? Will you commit to doing these things this week?

2. Read Matthew 6:33: "Seek first His kingdom and His righteousness, and all these things will be added to you."

Reflect

What does it mean to seek God's kingdom and righteousness?

Are you willing to put all of your eggs in one basket by putting God first and trusting that He will provide for all of your needs? Name one or two things you can do or not do this week to demonstrate this willingness.

3. Read John 15:5: "I am the vine, you are the branches; he who abides in Me and I in him, he bears much fruit, for apart from Me you can do nothing."

Reflect

What does it mean to abide in Christ?

What is the result of this abiding? What is the result of a lack of abiding?

How can abiding in Jesus help you overcome some of the challenges you're presently facing? Are you willing to commit to abiding in Him at an even greater level than you currently do or have ever done? Ask God to give you wisdom on how to do this. If you wish, write your prayer here.

4. Read 2 Corinthians 8:5: "They first gave themselves to the Lord and to us by the will of God."

Reflect
What does it look like to give yourself to the Lord?

How do you see giving yourself to the Lord spilling over into giving yourself to others?

Are you willing to increase how much of your time, talents, and treasures—and your thoughts—are given to the Lord and, consequently, to others? If so, what practical steps toward that commitment can you take this week? Record them here.

5. Review Revelation 2:5: "Remember from where you have fallen, and repent and do the deeds you did at first; or else I am coming to you and will remove your lampstand out of its place—unless you repent."

Reflect

What do you think it means for your lampstand to be removed from its place?

When have you been most intimate with God? If that time isn't now, repent of falling away from Him, and then determine if you're willing to return to Him and place Him first in every area of your life. If you wish, write your prayer here.

Ask God to reveal where He's not first in your life. As He brings these thoughts to your mind, ask Him for the strength and wisdom to put Him first in every way. If you wish, write your prayer here.

EXHIBITING STEADY FAITHFULNESS

COMMIT TO MEMORY

Thus says the LORD, the King of Israel and his Redeemer, the LORD of hosts: "I am the first and I am the last, and there is no God besides Me" (Isaiah 44:6).

CONSIDER

Before we move into a time of connecting, take in these key insights gleaned from Tony Evans and the *Living as an Overcomer* book. They set the stage for the rest of the session.

You might be familiar with the story of Brer Rabbit, a popular children's tale about a rabbit who's caught by a sly fox. The fox has tried to catch the also-sly rabbit for a long time, and yet once he does, he still has some catching to do.

The fox tells Brer Rabbit he's going to skin him and cook him in a stew, but Brer Rabbit has an answer the fox doesn't expect. Rather than being frightened of being skinned alive and boiled in a pot for lunch, Brer Rabbit pleads with the fox to not throw him into the briar patch. Even when the fox tells Brer Rabbit he's going to tear him from limb to limb, Brer Rabbit calmly responds, saying he can deal with that. But what he can't deal with is being thrown into the briar patch.

Eventually, this conversation winds down to a decision, and the fox concludes that the very worst thing he can do to inflict pain on Brer Rabbit is to throw him into the briar patch. So that's what he determines to do. But the crafty fox doesn't know Brer Rabbit has tricked him. He was born in the briar patch. He grew up in the briar patch. So in the fox's attempt to inflict greater suffering on Brer Rabbit, he actually casts him straight into a blessing.

What does this tale have to do with overcoming? A lot, as it gives us a perspective on Satan's attempts to harm and test us. Satan may tell you he plans to skin you alive, ruin your lives, and destroy you, but remember that God is greater than our enemy.

The beautiful thing about being a believer in Christ is that God is crafty enough to allow Satan to believe he's throwing you to your demise, but he's actually throwing you straight into God's hands. God can take the needles of the briar patch—the pricks of life—and turn them into something glorious. He can take what looks worse than bad and make it beautiful.

In Christ, you are an overcomer even in the midst of thorns, thistles, and trials. An overcomer is someone who takes their position in Christ and makes it their practice in Christ. It's not someone *trying* to overcome; it's someone who recognizes that they've *already* overcome. They're only in the process of working out the overcoming in their day-to-day life.

The church in Smyrna was located some 35 miles from the one in Ephesus. Smyrna was a well-known city with buildings constructed and erected in the form of a crown because it was one of the cities in Asia that had focused on emperor worship. The Christians there were undergoing a great deal of tribulation and trial, because they were disciples and not secretive about their faith.

Because of their troubles, Jesus introduces Himself to them in this manner: "The first and the last, who was dead, and has come to life" (Revelation 2:8). In light of what He's about to say to the church in Smyrna, Jesus makes a point of letting them know that He's the one who was dead but is now alive. If anyone were to understand troubles and trials, then, it would be Jesus.

Jesus knows that even though the church in Smyrna is going through a horrific time of tribulation, His call to faithfulness despite their circumstances is possible. He has done it. So He proceeds to tell them not to let their circumstances have the last word of their existence and not to let their problems become their God. They are not to deify their difficulties, but rather to dignify their difficulties by submitting them under the Lordship of Christ.

The beautiful thing about Jesus Christ is that He can relate to our troubles.

He can relate to us from up above as God, but He can also relate to us down here on earth. He went through pain and suffering, even to the point of death, and He remained obedient to His Father in it all. This is why Christ introduces Himself to the church in Smyrna by identifying Himself as the One who died but was also raised. Before He discusses their problems, He wants them to know that death does not have the last word.

Now, that doesn't mean there's no grave, but overcoming means the grave does not have the final say. Overcoming means your problem is not the bottom line. Overcoming means what you see is not what you get. It means that Calvary Friday is overruled by Resurrection Sunday. And whatever death you may be facing right now, whether a death in your circumstances, a relationship, your career, your finances, your health, or your emotions—or even in your dreams— Jesus wants you to know that He has the final word on all of it. He has the final word because He is the first, and He is the last. He has died, but He has also risen—indeed.

Excerpted from chapter 3, *Living as an Overcomer*

CONNECT

After praying together, respond to these suggestions or questions, remembering that sharing is part of connecting with others.

1. What did you learn or what stood out to you in your personal time in the Word since our last session?

2. What are some of the steps you're putting into practice based on the principles learned in this study so far? Have you noticed any positive outcomes? If so, what are they?

3. What has been your greatest struggle in applying some of the principles from our study thus far?

CAPTURE

Settle back and watch Tony's video teaching, taking in what he's been led to share for this session. The next section will help you unpack what you hear.

CONCENTRATE

The following questions, suggestions, and Scripture passages are designed to guide your discussion in response to Tony's teaching in the video.

Read Revelation 2:8-9: "The first and the last, who was dead, and has come to life, says this: 'I know your tribulation and your poverty (but you are rich), and the blasphemy by those who say they are Jews and are not, but are a synagogue of Satan.'"

1. What does Jesus say He knows about the people of the church in Smyrna?

2. Why do you think Jesus says the church members are actually rich even though He just said He knows their poverty?

3. In what ways can a person be spiritually rich yet materially poor?

Read Revelation 2:10: "Do not fear what you are about to suffer. Behold, the devil is about to cast some of you into prison, so that you will be tested, and you will have tribulation for ten days. Be faithful until death, and I will give you the crown of life."

1. What are the people of the church in Smyrna about to face?

2. What does Jesus urge them not to do in light of their pending suffering?

3. How difficult is it not to fear when you know you're about to face suffering?

4. What are some things we can do or thoughts we can have to help dissolve fear in the face of current or upcoming troubles?

5. In Revelation 2:10, we read that the tribulation for this church will last ten days. What does this time frame reveal?

6. Does knowing that Satan has a leash and that God is sovereign over all help give you courage when facing trials or tribulations? In what way does this truth bring you comfort?

CONVERGE

Explore how what you've learned in this session can converge with your daily life—in other words, how you can apply it. As you discuss the following, jot down personal notes and proposed actions in the extra space provided.

1. Describe a time when you thought the Lord was allowing testing and trials for some reason only He knew. What gave you the strength to continue in faith during this time?

2. What are some things you can do to encourage others who may be going through a season of testing or trial? What are some things you probably shouldn't do or say?

3. Read Revelation 2:11: "He who has an ear, let him hear what the Spirit says to the churches. He who overcomes will not be hurt by the second death." This verse speaks of what is obtained when overcoming trials and tribulations brought on by Satan. What does it mean to not be hurt by the "second death"?

4. Read Lamentations 3:22-24. In what ways have you experienced the Lord's mercy in times of drought or in life's valleys? What does it mean to you personally that the Lord is your portion? How can that truth help strengthen you to overcome adverse oppositions you may be facing in your life now or sometime in the future?

5. Read James 1:2-4. This passage brings us back to the concept of "wholeness" and "completeness" with regard to the number seven. Based on this Scripture, what do trials produce in us? Have you seen a progression in your maturity to steadfastly handle trials and tests that would have been too much for you in the past? How does it make you feel to witness your own personal growth toward wholeness?

CONCLUDE

To close the session, first worship the Lord together in any way meaningful to the group, such as singing a song. Then before a final prayer, share any prayer requests or praise for answered prayer.

CONTINUE

This last section is for you to use on your own over the next week, proceeding through the five opportunities for reflection as you wish—perhaps one per day. Before you work through the Scripture and questions, ask the Lord to open your ears to truly hear His truth and for His help in applying it in your life. Then record what He reveals to you in the extra space provided.

1. Read Isaiah 26:3-4: "The steadfast of mind You will keep in perfect peace, because he trusts in You. Trust in the LORD forever, for in GOD the LORD, we have an everlasting Rock."

   ### Reflect

   Based on this passage, what are we guaranteed is a result of the trials designed to promote steadfastness in our lives? What does that result look like in your life?

   Are you required to keep yourself in perfect peace? Or does God do this? Explain.

   What is your part to play in living as an overcomer who experiences perfect peace?

2. Read John 14:27: "Peace I leave with you; My peace I give to you; not as the world gives do I give to you. Do not let your heart be troubled, nor let it be fearful."

Reflect

What two things are we not to allow our hearts to be?

1.

2.

How is Christ's peace different from the peace the world gives?

Peace is priceless. How can you align your thoughts and mindsets under God at a greater level than you already are in order to tap into His gift of peace?

3. Read Psalm 27:5-6: "In the day of trouble He will conceal me in His tabernacle; in the secret place of His tent He will hide me; He will lift me up on a rock. And now my head will be lifted up above my enemies around me, and I will offer in His tent sacrifices with shouts of joy; I will sing, yes, I will sing praises to the LORD."

Reflect

What three things does this passage say the Lord will do for you on the day of trouble?

1.

2.

3.

What is to be your response when He does this for you?

Have you ever experienced a deeper intimacy with God during a trial than while life was going well for you? How does having a mindset that acknowledges this opportunity ahead of time help you mentally and emotionally prepare for a trial you may someday face?

4. Read 2 Corinthians 1:8-9: "We do not want you to be unaware, brethren, of our affliction which came to us in Asia, that we were burdened excessively, beyond our strength, so that we despaired even of life; indeed, we had the sentence of death within ourselves so that we would not trust in ourselves, but in God who raises the dead."

Reflect
Does it surprise you that the apostle Paul despaired of life—or in our contemporary language, was suicidal? Why or why not?

What was God teaching Paul and his companions during this severe time of testing?

Jesus introduces Himself to the church in Smyrna as the One who died but who was also raised from the dead. Paul refers to trusting in God who raises the dead as the lesson he learned from his tribulation. How does the reality that nothing is final unless God says it is give you strength to face the trials and tests you may be in now or may be in one day?

5. Review Isaiah 44:6: "Thus says the LORD, the King of Israel and his Redeemer, the Lord of hosts: 'I am the first and I am the last, and there is no God besides Me.'"

Reflect

What do you think God means when He refers to Himself as the first and the last?

How does the truth of God's preeminence over all affect the way you view your personal challenges?

Since there's no god besides the one true God, what does He deserve from you?

What is the greatest way you can tap into God's highest power available to help you overcome difficulties?

EMBRACING UNCOMPROMISING COMMITMENT

COMMIT TO MEMORY

He who has an ear, let him hear what the Spirit says to the churches. To him who overcomes, to him I will give some of the hidden manna, and I will give him a white stone, and a new name written on the stone which no one knows but he who receives it (Revelation 2:17).

CONSIDER

Before we move into a time of connecting, take in these key insights gleaned from Tony Evans and the *Living as an Overcomer* book. They set the stage for the rest of the session.

Have you ever driven behind someone on the highway who wasn't quite sure which lane they wanted to travel in? Sometimes they'd drive in your lane. Other times they'd move into another lane. To say that this person was indecisive would be an understatement.

The driver is obviously confused, and now everyone behind them is confused. Whenever someone is unstable about which way they're going, they inevitably create instability for others as well.

When Jesus introduces Himself to the church in Pergamum, 45 miles north of Smyrna, He does it as the One who holds the sharp two-edged sword. The two-edged sword refers to the Word of God, which can cut on both sides. Scripture can bring blessings, but it can also bring judgment. God's Word is good for both constructing and destructing things, depending on your relationship to it.

But because God's Word was being compromised in Pergamum, where much deception was going on, Jesus' message was graphic and straight to the point. In fact, Pergamum was the Washington, DC, of Satanism, the capital of the satanic. Revelation 2:13 reads, "I know where you dwell, where Satan's throne is; and you hold fast My name, and did not deny My faith even in the days of Antipas, My witness, My faithful one, who was killed among you, where Satan dwells."

The church in Smyrna had similar surroundings. They were said to be dwelling in the "synagogue of Satan" (Revelation 2:9). But here Jesus states that Pergamum is located smack-dab in the center of Satan's throne room. And in this dire predicament, He has a message about overcoming, about how to live above the culture, chaos, and quagmire around us.

He says the key to experiencing eternal victory in the midst of an earthly experience that's not so ideal comes in one word: commitment. He says if the people of the church at Pergamum (as well as us through the reading of Scripture) want to overcome, they must be uncompromising Christians. No believer can compromise, because compromise and commitment can't coexist.

The driver I mentioned earlier can't simultaneously compromise on which lane they drive in while also committing to a certain lane. It has to be one or the other, because the two are mutually exclusive. Jesus says commitment must be the goal, especially with those who are surrounded by an enormous amount of compromise.

Satan's method of rule is always steeped in deception. He gives us the wrong direction and the wrong pathway, and he does it in such a way as to deceive. Satan's power is rooted in deception and manipulation. That's why he tries to steer us away from God's Word. The further we're away from God's Word, the easier we can be deceived. God's Word is truth and like a lamp that guides us to know truth. So Satan has to separate believers from the Word of God in order to deceive.

There's a great crisis in our own culture today—the absence and questioning of God's Word. The absence of God's Word began decades ago as our culture started to pull away from the integration of Scripture throughout society. But the questioning of God's Word and its validity has grown stronger in recent years as the debate over what is truth—and whose truth is the real truth—has become prevalent. This is what happened to the church in Pergamum. They had drifted far enough from the Word of God to become ensnared in deception.

Satan knows if he can get you to think the wrong thoughts, they will eventually show up in your behavior. If he can get your mind away from the truth of God's Word, he can much more easily deceive you into spiritual compromise and lethargy. He can move you away from the favor of God and keep you from experiencing life as an overcomer.

It doesn't take much more than a cursory glance around us to recognize this strategy of Satan's today. We see it on social media, in various streaming and TV programming, and in the way the culture is seeking to redefine Christian values. Our public schools are frequently turning into a place of secular indoctrination. Our societal discourse is littered with deception and accusation. Even the spiritual leaders and pastors in our churches are compromising the Word of God to satisfy the societal environment instead of teaching truth.

Jesus both condemned the church in Pergamum for their failings and told them what they needed to do:

> I have a few things against you, because you have there some who hold the teaching of Balaam, who kept teaching Balak to put a stumbling block before the sons of Israel, to eat things sacrificed to idols and to commit acts of immorality. So you also have some who in the same way hold the teaching of the Nicolaitans. Therefore repent; or else I am coming to you quickly, and I will make war against them with the sword of My mouth (Revelation 2:14-16).

Only through repentance could the church in Pergamum overcome Satan's hook of deception. And only through repentance and returning to God's Word can we do the same.

Excerpted from chapter 4, *Living as an Overcomer*

CONNECT

After praying together, respond to these suggestions or questions, remembering that sharing is part of connecting with others.

1. What stood out to you in your personal time in the Word since our last session?

2. How have you recently witnessed God's hand in your circumstances and challenges?

CAPTURE

Settle back and watch Tony's video teaching, taking in what he's been led to share for this session. The next section will help you unpack what you hear.

CONCENTRATE

The following questions, suggestions, and Scripture passages are designed to guide your discussion in response to Tony's teaching in the video.

Read Revelation 2:12-17.

1. Describe the cultural surroundings the members of the church in Pergamum must have lived in.

2. Contrast that with the culture we live in today, as well as with some other cultures abroad.

3. Why do you think Antipas lost his life (verse 13)?

4. Do you think we're moving toward a point in our culture when even loss of life for being a Christian could be expected? How challenging might it be to stay committed to Christ if we were at that point?

5. In the video, Tony explains what the compromise of Balaam was. Discuss what that looked like and whether this type of compromise is happening in our Christian culture today.

6. Tony shares that Jesus is calling the church to repent and become people of conviction. Name some convictions that have become compromised in our Christian culture today. How can we personally return to living in light of their full conviction?

7. Describe what, according to the teaching we heard, the "white stone" could entail as a reward.

CONVERGE

Explore how what you've learned in this session can converge with your daily life—in other words, how you can apply it. As you discuss the following, jot down personal notes and proposed action steps in the extra space provided.

1. Describe a time when your Christian values were challenged by the culture or people around you. How did you respond? Do you think you should have responded any differently?

2. How does a commitment to convictions help us in overcoming the challenges we face?

3. Read Revelation 2:17: "He who has an ear, let him hear what the Spirit says to the churches. To him who overcomes, to him I will give some of the hidden manna, and I will give him a white stone, and a new name written on the stone which no one knows but he who receives it."

Discuss what you think the white stone and new name represent. In what way would this special, intimate relationship with Jesus Christ improve your life not only on earth but also in eternity?

4. Sometimes our convictions may differ from others. First Corinthians 10:28 says, "If anyone says to you, 'This is meat sacrificed to idols,' do not eat it, for the sake of the one who informed you, and for conscience' sake." Discuss what Paul's admonition is regarding our freedoms and convictions when they intersect with other people's. What might be examples of this today?

5. Is there an area in your life where you feel convicted to increase your commitment and decrease your compromise? Specifics aren't necessary, but allow some time to discuss this if anyone wants to share, perhaps asking to be remembered in prayer.

CONCLUDE

To close the session, first worship the Lord together in any way meaningful to the group, such as singing a song. Then before a final prayer, share any prayer requests or praise for answered prayer.

CONTINUE

This last section is for you to use on your own over the next week, proceeding through the five opportunities for reflection as you wish—perhaps one per day. Before you work through the

Scripture and questions, ask the Lord to open your ears to truly hear His truth and for His help in applying it in your life. Then record what He reveals to you in the extra space provided.

1. Read Hebrews 10:26: "If we go on sinning willfully after receiving the knowledge of the truth, there no longer remains a sacrifice for sins."

   Reflect
   What does this verse mean to you?

   Is there an area in your life where God has convicted you about a particular sin but you have not yet responded to Him? Are you willing to respond now in light of this truth? If you wish, write your response in prayer here.

2. Read John 14:15: "If you love Me, you will keep My commandments."

   Reflect
   What should be our motivation for living a life of purity?

   Does your love for Jesus Christ motivate you to keep His commandments? Or does something else motivate you, such as legalism, pride, or fear of consequences? Describe what's holding you back from a commitment to the principles of a Christian life.

How can you seek to increase your love for Jesus Christ? Ask God for wisdom on how to cultivate this love relationship even more. If you wish, write your prayer here.

3. Read Colossians 3:5: "Consider the members of your earthly body as dead to immorality, impurity, passion, evil desire, and greed, which amounts to idolatry."

Reflect
Does it surprise you to read the word *greed* in this list of sins? Why or why not?

In what ways does greed show up in both our contemporary Christian culture today and your own life?

Do you need to make some changes in order to live a purer life in Christ? Ask God for wisdom on how to cease ongoing sins and guard yourself from adopting any in the future. If you wish, write you prayer here. Then be sure to record here or in a journal what the Spirit tells you in your times of prayer or throughout your days in response to your request.

4. Read Proverbs 25:28: "Like a city that is broken into and without walls is a man who has no control over his spirit."

Reflect

What does it mean to have no control over your spirit?

What are the areas where you feel you have a lack of control or less control over your spirit?

In what ways can you adjust your thoughts, mindsets, and choices to have better control over your spirit?

5. Review Revelation 2:17: "He who has an ear, let him hear what the Spirit says to the churches. To him who overcomes, to him I will give some of the hidden manna, and I will give him a white stone, and a new name written on the stone which no one knows but he who receives it."

Reflect

What does the "hidden manna" mean to you?

How has this session on overcoming convicted you?

How can you share what you've learned with others in your spheres of influence?

Make a commitment to pray for greater conviction in your life and a greater outgrowth of your love for Christ.

VIEWING SIN GOD'S WAY

COMMIT TO MEMORY

You are from God, little children, and have overcome them; because greater is He who is in you than he who is in the world (1 John 4:4).

CONSIDER

Before we move into a time of connecting, take in these key insights gleaned from Tony Evans and the *Living as an Overcomer* book. They set the stage for the rest of the session.

If you've been to an airport to travel, then you know what a magnetometer is. You have to go through one in order to pass through security. It may feel like an inconvenience, but it's actually part of the process set in place to protect you. The magnetometer alerts personnel to anything considered unacceptable or may be damaging and destructive on your flight. It searches out that which may be hidden in order to identify it before it can bring anyone harm.

Thyatira was located 45 miles southwest of Pergamum and known for its unions related to work. At that time, not only did the unions represent a work environment but they had a particular god associated with it. To be a part of the union or guild, you needed to declare allegiance to the false god. So when Jesus speaks to the church in Thyatira, He brings up these hidden associations like a magnetometer would.

At first He commends them for the good they're doing. But then the sin they're tolerating in their midst is pointed out. While they may not be participating in the evil themselves, their act of accepting the evil of another is unveiled. Revelation 2:19-20 says:

> I know your deeds, and your love and faith and service and perseverance, and that your deeds of late are greater than at first. But I have this against you, that you tolerate the woman Jezebel, who calls herself a prophetess, and she teaches and leads My bond-servants astray so that they commit acts of immorality and eat things sacrificed to idols.

The interesting thing about this church is that they're not necessarily being judged for what they're doing wrong themselves but for allowing certain things to take place within their midst. They were being judged for a particular problem that had infiltrated the church and the Christian community there.

Although Jezebel of the Bible was long dead at this point, this woman Jesus called Jezebel was a self-appointed leader in the church who was wreaking havoc among the congregation by advocating a false doctrine. Jezebel was promoting idolatry and immorality. Her influence had penetrated this small group of believers so that they were being compromised in their commitment and in their faith. This hidden compromise caused a decline in the spiritual vitality of the church as well as the unity with Jesus Christ.

Tolerating sin can be just as bad as committing it, depending on the circumstances. Jesus wanted them to know that this compromise was detrimental to their spiritual well-being. The solution came only through a call to repentance. Tolerating spiritual compromise in your own life is detrimental to your spiritual well-being too. A call to repentance is always a call to reversal in both thought and direction. God will not tolerate compromise. He has no tolerance for sin.

One of the reasons living in America is so enticing to people around the world is that even with all of its flaws and weaknesses, there's the opportunity for advancement. The structure of our nation offers each of us the chance to take an idea and maximize it, within appropriate boundaries, for growth. This is why we live in a continually competitive environment, where if someone else comes up with a better concept than ours and positions it more strategically, it will either force us to improve or cause us to go under.

Because of this, one of the standards many corporations have adopted is this concept of zero tolerance. Zero tolerance states there's little or no room for error. In other words, to maximize business productivity, we must decrease our level of tolerance for error. In being human, we will never perfectly reach that, but if it is the goal, it will set a business and product apart, because when mediocrity is the standard, people will simply shop elsewhere.

Now, if that's true with regard to maximizing your potential as an American, would it not equally be true to maximize your potential as a Christian? If sinful customers still want an excellent product, then isn't it logical that a perfect God would want a good return as well? If sinful men will be ticked off at paying for mediocrity in either an item or performance, then should we not understand how a perfect God would be less than satisfied when we settle for less than our best as believers?

Zero tolerance means just that—zero tolerance. We accept this reality in many areas of our lives, and yet we far too often question it when it comes to God's standard, His view of morality. Yet is God to expect less from you and me—and from His church? In order for the body of Christ to live as overcomers both on earth and for eternity, we need to live with a zero tolerance mindset toward sin. Far too many of us live as victims today rather than victors, and one of the main reasons is that we tolerate too much that doesn't reflect the values of the kingdom of God either in ourselves or in others.

Excerpted from chapter 5, *Living as an Overcomer*

CONNECT

After praying together, respond to these suggestions or questions, remembering that sharing is part of connecting with others.

1. Reflect on our overall study of overcoming so far. Share any new insights you've learned and perhaps applied in your life since our last session.

2. In what ways has this study met your expectations? In what ways has it differed?

3. Out of all of the churches we've looked at so far, which one resonates the most with you—and why?

CAPTURE

Settle back and watch Tony's video teaching, taking in what he's been led to share for this session. The next section will help you unpack what you hear.

CONCENTRATE

The following questions, suggestions, and Scripture passages are designed to guide your discussion in response to Tony's teaching in the video.

Read Revelation 2:18-28.

1. Had everyone in the church in Thyatira committed rebellion in tolerating the deeds of this Jezebel? Explain.

2. What is the message to those who had not been tolerant of this sin?

3. What is the message to those who had tolerated this Jezebel's rebellious deeds? According to Revelation 2:18-28, were they to repent of their own sins, hers, or both?

4. Why do you think this church is told to repent of someone else's deeds?

5. Read Job 1:4-5. What is Job doing on behalf of his children?

6. In the video, Tony speaks of this Jezebel's position as one reason she was able to get away with so much immoral behavior and enticement. How does a position of spiritual authority sometimes impact whether we choose to hold someone accountable within the body of Christ? Should things be this way? If not, what can be done to address it?

7. One of the things this Jezebel did was encourage people to eat things sacrificed to idols. Tony defines idolatry as any person, place, thought, or thing that usurps God's rightful rule in your life. What are some of the idols we have in our contemporary

American culture, such as materialism or narcissism? In what ways are we tolerating and even embracing these idols in the body of Christ?

CONVERGE

Explore how what you've learned in this session can converge with your daily life—in other words, how you can apply it. As you discuss the following, jot down personal notes and proposed action steps in the extra space provided.

1. Describe a situation where in hindsight you felt you compromised your Christian beliefs or values and later experienced the consequences. It's fine to speak in generic terms about what the Lord taught you through this or any situation without specific details.

2. Do you think the standard should or could be raised higher anywhere in your life or relationships? If it's not too personal, share this with the group.

3. How does knowing the rewards of overcoming give you motivation to repent of your sins, overcome temptation, and not tolerate the sinful influences of others?

4. Accountability is tricky, because it sometimes feels like uninvited judgment. Discuss how you can be more willing to be held accountable for sins you may not even recognize you're committing. Share some best practices that have worked for you or others in the past.

CONCLUDE

To close the session, first worship the Lord together in any way meaningful to the group, such as singing a song. Then before a final prayer, share any prayer requests or praise for answered prayer.

CONTINUE

This last section is for you to use on your own over the next week, proceeding through the five opportunities for reflection as you wish—perhaps one per day. Before you work through the Scripture and questions, ask the Lord to open your ears to truly hear His truth and for His help in applying it in your life. Then record what He reveals to you in the extra space provided.

1. Read Galatians 2:20: "I have been crucified with Christ; and it is no longer I who live, but Christ lives in me; and the life which I now live in the flesh I live by faith in the Son of God, who loved me and gave Himself up for me."

Reflect
From a practical standpoint, what does it mean for Christ to live in you?

In what ways do you experience the truth that you've been crucified with Christ and now live by faith in the Son of God? How do you believe you could experience this at a greater level?

Commit Galatians 2:20 to memory, then make a habit of saying it each morning as you start your day in order to align your mindset under Christ's authority and rule.

> I have been crucified with Christ; and it is no longer I who live, but Christ lives in me; and the life which I now live in the flesh I live by faith in the Son of God, who loved me and gave Himself up for me (Galatians 2:20).

2. Read 1 Corinthians 10:13: "No temptation has overtaken you but such as is common to man; and God is faithful, who will not allow you to be tempted beyond what you are able, but with the temptation will provide the way of escape also, so that you will be able to endure it."

Reflect

Are you facing a temptation in your life right now? Can you identify the "way of escape"? If not, ask the Lord for wisdom on where or what this is. If you wish, write your prayer here.

Consider Christ's suffering on the cross, which He endured for the joy set before Him. Are you willing to endure rather than act on temptation in order to gain the eternal reward Jesus spoke of in His message to the church in Thyatira? Why or why not?

Reflect on a temptation you gave in to and the consequences that ensued. What did these consequences teach you?

3. Read Revelation 12:11: "They overcame him because of the blood of the Lamb and because of the word of their testimony, and they did not love their life even when faced with death."

Reflect

Revelation 12:11 tells us "the brethren" overcame because of the blood of the Lamb and the word of their testimony. What is your testimony that will enable you to overcome further temptation or trial? Record it here.

How does the blood of the Lamb ensure our ability to overcome? Explain.

What should we not love more than we love the Lord? Explain.

Do you struggle with loving your life more than surrendering to the Lord in a spirit of love for Him? In what way does this show up the most?

4. Read 1 John 4:1: "Beloved, do not believe every spirit, but test the spirits to see whether they are from God, because many false prophets have gone out into the world."

   ### Reflect
   What does it mean to test the spirits?

   Is it easy to spot a false prophet in our contemporary Christian culture? What are some of the indicators?

   How often are you to test the spirits to see whether they're from God? Aligning your thoughts with the truth of God's Word is one way of discerning whether what you're thinking is from God. Do you make this a regular practice? If not, will you commit to doing so? Record a commitment you're willing to make here.

5. Review 1 John 4:4: "You are from God, little children, and have overcome them; because greater is He who is in you than he who is in the world."

   ### Reflect
   What do you think "greater is He who is in you than he who is in the world" means?

If you're struggling with tolerance and temptation, what is one thing you can do to strengthen your resolve to overcome?

How do you personally tap into and abide in the presence of Jesus Christ?

Are you willing to seek to increase your abiding in Christ so that you'll have a greater access to His power in you? Ask the Lord for wisdom on how to do that. If you wish, write your prayer here.

WALKING IN THE SPIRIT'S POWER

COMMIT TO MEMORY

Thus says the Lord to the house of Israel, "Seek Me that you may live" (Amos 5:4).

CONSIDER

Before we move into a time of connecting, take in these key insights gleaned from Tony Evans and the *Living as an Overcomer* book. They set the stage for the rest of the session.

Have you ever ordered a steak well done only to discover it's still rare inside—or witnessed someone else experience this? Usually, the first cut into the steak is followed by a conversation with the person waiting on your table. The plate is swiftly taken to the kitchen for more heat, and then when it's returned, the person waits to be sure the inside now matches expectation.

This illustrates the problem with the church in Sardis, located roughly 30 miles east of Smyrna and 30 miles southeast of Thyatira. It was a major garment district servicing the nearby communities.

Externally, the church looked the part of committed, spiritual, biblically based believers. They resembled those who lived out the truth of God's Word and His principles. But on the inside, that was not their reality.

One look beneath the surface and you could easily see they did not hold to the faith they claimed so loudly publicly. They had fallen prey to a spiritual condition of complacency, and this, in turn, had affected and infected them. What they portrayed to the public was not who they truly were before God. And as a result, they had a reputation that did not reflect their spiritual reality. The church in Sardis could be what we might call "gold-plated Christians." They had the look of spiritual greatness without any real connection to God on the inside.

Thus, the Lord had to confront them and call them to repent and wake up. He wanted to jar them from their spiritual stupor and complacency:

> I know your deeds, that you have a name that you are alive, but you are dead. Wake up, and strengthen the things that remain, which were about to die; for I have not found your deeds completed in the sight of My God. So remember what you have received and heard; and keep it, and repent. Therefore if you do not wake up, I will come like a thief, and you will not know at what hour I will come to you (Revelation 3:1-3).

Jesus seeks to rouse them from their spiritual lethargy and slumber. He warns them that if they don't wake up, He will come to them in a way that will severely discipline them. No one enjoys being woken up to discipline. But that's what Jesus says He will do if they don't choose to wake up on their own. He will do it out of a heart of love and concern, not to be mean.

In their slumber, they had forgotten their dependence on God. They had become self-reliant. They had become focused only on their own material gains and provision. They had lost sight of God and His rightful place in their lives and in their church. The root of their problem was that they had become so self-sufficient in their own minds that they didn't feel they needed the Holy Spirit anymore. They thought they could do everything on their own, which is a very dangerous place to be.

Do you know why Christians don't seek God more than we do? Because too many of us are too self-sufficient. We don't feel like we need God until an emergency shows up. The Christians in Sardis were educated, affluent, and at ease, and as a result, they relied too heavily on themselves and became blind to the enemy's surprise attacks.

One of the greatest dangers of success—whether it's financial, relational, or anything else—is that the higher you go up the ladder, the more independent you become. Success often lends itself to a spirit of independence that involves God only in periods of crisis.

But not only were the Christians in Sardis self-sufficient, so were the pastors and spiritual leaders. We know this because Jesus had introduced Himself as the One who has the seven stars, and stars are a reference to the spiritual leaders. This reveals that there was a void of quality leadership in the church. The leadership that should have been setting the pace for the congregation to follow in terms of grabbing onto and pursuing the work of the Spirit had been setting the wrong pace of independence and ease.

The job of the Holy Spirit is not only to energize your spiritual life but to make sure Satan doesn't have his way with you. It's to give you victory to overcome. But the Holy Spirit doesn't do His work apart from your connection and cooperation to Him and with Him. A life devoid of the Spirit of God is a life open to defeat in every area. It's in the power of the Spirit that you are able to overcome.

Excerpted from chapter 6, *Living as an Overcomer*

CONNECT

After praying together, respond to these suggestions or questions, remembering that sharing is part of connecting with others.

1. Share a time you experienced the Lord's unique presence in your life since we last met.

2. How has the Holy Spirit been speaking to you with regard to the principles we're studying?

3. Were you able to share what you've been learning in this study with anyone else? If so, how was it received?

4. Which church do you find yourself identifying with the most thus far? Why?

CAPTURE

Settle back and watch Tony's video teaching, taking in what he's been led to share for this session. The next section will help you unpack what you hear.

CONCENTRATE

The following questions, suggestions, and Scripture passages are designed to guide your discussion in response to Tony's teaching in the video.

Read Revelation 3:1-6.

1. The church in Sardis had a great reputation, and their name referred to their reputation. It had all of the trappings of a church that was "happening." But what was lacking?

2. Is it possible to be well known for being spiritual yet simultaneously be spiritually dead in God's economy? What are some things or thoughts that can lead to this state?

3. What is the primary role of the Holy Spirit? How does He go about fulfilling this role?

4. Tony tells us that the spiritual had become secondary to the secular for the people of the church in Sardis. Give some examples of how this might be happening today in the overall body of Christ.

5. The members of the church in Sardis were told to "wake up." What were they to do once they did?

CONVERGE

Explore how what you've learned in this session can converge with your daily life—in other words, how you can apply it. As you discuss the following, jot down personal notes and proposed action steps in the extra space provided.

1. Describe how the struggles of the church in Sardis may be common to the contemporary church in America today. How do they differ?

2. Do you experience an increase in your spiritual fervency and prayer life when your days are rocky? If so, why do you think this happens?

3. What can you do to increase your fervency even in times of calm?

4. The teaching this week references special rewards in eternity not everyone will be allowed to experience. Describe how you feel when you think of attending special events in eternity. Is it difficult to wrap your mind around what this might be like? Why or why not?

5. How can this truth motivate you to pursue God passionately while you're still on earth?

6. The Bible instructs us to encourage one another. Yet in this message to the church in Sardis, we discover that too many compliments may lead to complacency. Discuss the tension between offering encouragement and going overboard. Is there such a thing as too much attention on any one person, activity, or church?

7. How can you apply the message to the church in Sardis to your own life? Offer tangible and practical examples that may also help someone else who's listening.

CONCLUDE

To close the session, first worship the Lord together in any way meaningful to the group, such as singing a song. Then before a final prayer, share any prayer requests or praise for answered prayer.

CONTINUE

This last section is for you to use on your own over the next week, proceeding through the five opportunities for reflection as you wish—perhaps one per day. Before you work through the Scripture and questions, ask the Lord to open your ears to truly hear His truth and for His help in applying it in your life. Then record what He reveals to you in the extra space provided.

1. Read 1 Chronicles 16:11: "Seek the LORD and His strength; seek His face continually."

Reflect

What should you do according to 1 Chronicles 16:11?

On a scale of 1 to 10 with 10 being the most, where do you rate yourself as seeking God continually? Practically speaking, how can you seek God continually?

In what ways can you benefit from having God's strength in your life and not relying only on your own? In what way can you gain more of His strength?

2. Read Hebrews 11:6: "Without faith it is impossible to please [God], for he who comes to God must believe that He is and that He is a rewarder of those who seek Him."

Reflect

What are some rewards you've experienced from the Lord?

Will spiritual rewards be made manifest only in heaven? Or do we receive them on earth as well? Explain.

In what ways can you demonstrate a greater faith in God through your actions? Has the Lord been convicting you to go deeper in your faith with Him in a particular area?

Think of at least one action step you can take to show God a deeper faith this week, being mindful of His presence as you seek Him more and more each day. Then record here or journal any personal moments the Lord gives you with Himself that are unique to your normal time with Him.

3. Read James 4:8: "Draw near to God and He will draw near to you. Cleanse your hands, you sinners; and purify your hearts, you double-minded."

Reflect

What does it mean to be double-minded?

In what ways do you find yourself being double-minded?

How can you develop a greater fervency for God and a greater focus on Him so that you will reduce any double-mindedness in your life? Will you commit to pursuing this fervency and focus?

4. Read Psalm 9:10: "Those who know Your name will put their trust in You, for You, O Lord, have not forsaken those who seek You."

Reflect

What are you promised if you seek God?

God will never forsake you when you seek Him. In what area of your life do you feel He's not very present right now? Record your commitment to seeking what He says about this in His Word and in prayer, later adding what you've learned.

5. Review Amos 5:4: "Thus says the LORD to the house of Israel, 'Seek Me that you may live.'"

Reflect

Have you experienced times when you've not sought the Lord as much as you could have? If so, what were the results?

If you're struggling with motivation to seek God more fervently, ask Him for wisdom and strength to do that. He promises to answer every prayer in alignment with His will, so pray in confidence that He will guide you closer to Him when you ask Him to do just that. If you wish, write a prayer here.

Do you believe that God can revive something that has died in your life—a relationship, a dream, an ambition, career status, or anything else you're dealing with? Seek the Lord and His favor for this particular area of your life. Ask Him to show you what you need to do to demonstrate your trust in Him. If you wish, write your prayer here.

Why is it important to seek God continually to live as an overcomer?

Tony has written two books on the names of God—*The Power of God's Names* and *Praying Through the Names of God*. Use these or other resources to uncover God's many characteristics in order to deepen your trust in Him.

ACCESSING SPIRITUAL AUTHORITY

COMMIT TO MEMORY

By their own sword they did not possess the land, and their own arm did not save them, but Your right hand and Your arm and the light of Your presence, for You favored them (Psalm 44:3).

CONSIDER

Before we move into a time of connecting, take in these key insights gleaned from Tony Evans and the *Living as an Overcomer* book. They set the stage for the rest of the session.

Sometimes airplanes crash because an invisible, powerful wind shear suddenly forces them downward with such pressure that they're unable to recover. These wind shears seem to come out of nowhere.

This is sort of like the trials in your life. You're flying along, minding your own business, doing the best you can, when suddenly, something unexpected impacts you negatively. Some burst of opposition forces you to crash in some way—even have a meltdown.

Technology called Doppler radar was developed to address wind shears for planes. This meteorological marvel sees the unseeable, reads it, and then lets pilots know what they may soon have to contend with. A wise pilot pays close attention to what the radar says, understanding that it can see and understand what a human being can't. A pilot would be a fool to trust only instincts and ignore this assistance.

Likewise, you and I are fools when we trust our instincts and ignore the One who can see the unseeable in our lives and help us make sense of what intends to make us crash. Unseen forces out there want to keep us from a safe landing.

The church in Philadelphia was not wealthy or powerful. They just didn't have all that much going for them, which is why Jesus begins His message to them with this reminder of who He is: "He who is holy, who is true, who has the key of David, who opens and no one will shut, and who shuts and no one opens" (Revelation 3:7).

The church had learned to live in true dependence on the Lord, not thinking too highly of themselves. They knew they were of "little power" and needed God's intervention. They had lived in light of their name, which meant "brotherly love."

The Christians in Philadelphia were a small body, but they weren't intimidated in living out their faith. They lived with full commitment to Christ, in both their worship and their words. They sought to preserve Christian values in the society and city in which they lived. And even though they faced great resistance by "the synagogue of Satan," they didn't bow down or cower in fear. Their faith was public, visible, and observable. As a result, they received the authority of Jesus Christ working on their behalf. And when we keep the Word like the saints in Philadelphia did, we can tap into this same authority.

Jesus said to them:

> I will cause those of the synagogue of Satan, who say that they are Jews and are not, but lie—I will make them come and bow down at your feet, and make them know that I have loved you. Because you have kept the word of My perseverance, I also will keep you from the hour of testing, that hour which is about to come upon the whole world, to test those who dwell on the earth (Revelation 3:9-10).

But Christians need to understand that Jesus doesn't have the same level of intimacy and relationship with all believers. We read about this in John 2:23-25:

> Now when He was in Jerusalem at the Passover, during the feast, many believed in His name, observing His signs which He was doing. But Jesus, on His part, was not entrusting Himself to them, for He knew all men, and

because He did not need anyone to testify concerning man, for He Himself knew what was in man.

In this passage John lets us know that many people believed in Jesus and had been saved. But because they weren't fully committed to Jesus, He also did not fully commit to them. See, being saved alone doesn't mean you're experiencing the full kingdom authority of Jesus. That comes only if you, like the Philadelphia church, go all in with God.

To go all in refers to consistently keeping God's Word. To honoring His name both internally and externally. When you do, you receive the benefits and blessings of God, allowing you to live as an overcomer. Jesus can shut down what's coming against you because He holds the keys.

At the church where I pastor, I have a master key that enables me to open any door at any time. All doors are subject to the master key. Individuals who work at the church have keys for their own individual spaces or offices, but they don't possess a master key.

This simple illustration reminds us that Jesus Christ has a master key to the universe. He's the One with full access to anything and everything. And if you keep His Word, you can tap into His kingdom authority when you call on Him. Jesus offers you this access when you live as a fully committed follower of His.

If you remain faithful to Jesus, He will be faithful to you, especially when you need Him most. You may not have a lot of worldly clout or influence, but if you know the King of kings and Lord of lords, you have access to all you will ever need. Never think you're somehow powerless just because you don't have all the extras some Christians or ministries have. If you know Jesus Christ intimately, you have access to all the spiritual authority you could ever need. Jesus can open doors that no man can open or keep closed. Just call on His name when you need to overcome. He will deliver you because you have lived a life of faithful commitment to Him.

Excerpted from chapter 7, *Living as an Overcomer*

CONNECT

After praying together, respond to these suggestions or questions, remembering that sharing is part of connecting with others.

1. What major thought or concept stands out to you from our last session?

2. How have you incorporated any principles we've learned into your daily life?

3. Has the Lord been speaking to you about any major life changes as a result of this study?

CAPTURE

Settle back and watch Tony's video teaching, taking in what he's been led to share for this session. The next section will help you unpack what you hear.

CONCENTRATE

The following questions, suggestions, and Scripture passages are designed to guide your discussion in response to Tony's teaching in the video.

1. Read Revelation 3:7-13. What are your overall thoughts related to the church in Philadelphia?

2. Read Psalm 110:1: "The LORD says to my Lord: 'Sit at My right hand until I make Your enemies a footstool for Your feet.'" What does it mean for your enemies to be made as your footstool?

3. Does Jesus mention anything He wants the church in Philadelphia to change?

4. What will Jesus make the "enemies" know about the people of the church in Philadelphia?

5. God is love. What do you think Jesus means when He says He will make others know that He has loved them? God loves everyone, but do even believers experience different levels of intimacy with God? How so?

6. Based on the video teaching, what was the example of special recognition Jesus said He will give to those in the church in Philadelphia if they "hold fast" to what they have?

CONVERGE

Explore how what you've learned in this session can converge with your daily life—in other words, how you can apply it. As you discuss the following, jot down personal notes and proposed action steps in the extra space provided.

1. Describe a time when you did "the right thing" and suffered consequences because of it, yet later saw God turn it around.

2. What role do faithfulness, obedience, and perseverance play in overcoming?

3. Read Revelation 3:12. Did you know that Jesus will be given a new name? What do you think this new name will entail or represent?

4. In the video teaching, Tony talks about what the church in Philadelphia had to overcome. Since they weren't judged for anything, what did they have to overcome? Keep in mind, it had to do with the fact that they had "little power."

5. Have you witnessed God promote you or someone you know who had "little power" by the world's standards and continue to open doors of influence and impact? What do you think set this person or yourself apart to receive this favor? What steps can you take to position yourself for God to open more doors for you?

CONCLUDE

To close the session, first worship the Lord together in any way meaningful to the group, such as singing a song. Then before a final prayer, share any prayer requests or praise for answered prayer.

CONTINUE

This last section is for you to use on your own over the next week, proceeding through the five opportunities for reflection as you wish—perhaps one per day. Before you work through the Scripture and questions, ask the Lord to open your ears to truly hear His truth and for His help in applying it in your life. Then record what He reveals to you in the extra space provided.

1. Read Proverbs 3:5-6: "Trust in the Lord with all your heart and do not lean on your own understanding. In all your ways acknowledge Him, and He will make your paths straight."

Reflect

What does it look like to you to "acknowledge" God?

Do you need to depend on God more than on your own understanding in any areas of your life? Which ones? Why do you think this is a challenge?

What does God do when we depend on Him for guidance and deliverance?

2. Read Psalm 121:1-2: "I will lift up my eyes to the mountains; from where shall my help come? My help comes from the LORD, who made heaven and earth."

Reflect

From where does your help come?

Since God made heaven and earth, will He have any trouble delivering you from whatever you're facing? Why or why not?

Are you trying to solve any specific part of your life rather than turning to God? What will you do to rectify this approach?

3. Read Isaiah 40:29: "He gives strength to the weary, and to him who lacks might He increases power."

Reflect

What does God do for the person who lacks might?

Are you fighting a battle that God wants you to give Him to fight for you? Will you turn it over? What action steps can you take to demonstrate that?

Ask the Lord to give you strength where you are weary and to confirm His strength in you this very week in an obvious manner. If you wish, write your prayer here.

4. Read 1 Chronicles 29:14: "Who am I and who are my people that we should be able to offer as generously as this? For all things come from You, and from Your hand we have given You."

Reflect

In what spirit is 1 Chronicles 29:14 written?

Do you carry a spirit of humility and gratitude for the things God has done for you and in you? Or do you have a measure of self-achievement and pride? Explain.

In what ways can you adjust your thoughts, mindsets, and choices to better reflect a spirit of utter dependency on the Lord?

5. Review Psalm 44:3: "By their own sword they did not possess the land, and their own arm did not save them, but Your right hand and Your arm and the light of Your presence, for You favored them."

Reflect

What does it look like to receive God's favor?

Are you seeking God's favor through your own obedience to Him? If not, why not?

In what way can you increase your obedience and dependence on God?

Thank the Lord for every door He's opened for you and every door He's shut to the enemy's attacks on you. If you wish, write your prayer here.

REFLECTING AUTHENTIC CHRISTIANITY

COMMIT TO MEMORY

Whoever wishes to save his life will lose it, but whoever loses his life for My sake, he is the one who will save it (Luke 9:24).

CONSIDER

Before we move into a time of connecting, take in these key insights gleaned from Tony Evans and the *Living as an Overcomer* book. They set the stage for the rest of the session.

We've come to our final church—the church in Laodicea. If Philadelphia is the obedient church whose members demonstrated the obedience of overcomers, then Laodicea is the exact opposite. Laodicea can best be described as an inauthentic church. It's made up of people who are in it for themselves. They obey when it brings them glory, but just as quickly they stab God in the back when it doesn't.

To say that Jesus is not a happy camper with the church in Laodicea would be a gross understatement. This neither hot nor cold church doesn't make our Savior shrug His shoulders or turn His head in disappointment. It makes Him want to vomit. It makes Him want to "spew" them right out of His mouth. He can't swallow because He can't even stomach them. They make Him gag.

We find the reason for His reaction in Revelation 3:17-18:

Because you say, "I am rich, and have become wealthy, and have need of nothing," and you do not know that you are wretched and miserable and poor and blind and naked, I advise you to buy from Me gold refined by fire so that you may become rich, and white garments so that you may clothe yourself, and that the shame of your nakedness will not be revealed; and eye salve to anoint your eyes so that you may see.

The town of Laodicea was well known. It was a popular town, very successful and wealthy. It had a positive reputation related to banking, clothing, and the pharmaceutical industry. They were well positioned geographically to service other communities, and in return, to benefit financially and become prosperous. But it was also their geography that revealed their spiritual weakness.

Jesus called them "lukewarm" because of the two rivers that flowed into Laodicea. One river flowed from Acropolis, and it was like the hot springs of Arkansas. Then from Colossi, cold water flowed down to them. When the two rivers joined, the water was neither hot nor cold. It was lukewarm. Jesus tapped into that geographical reality to reveal this church's spiritual calamity.

Who doesn't like a hot tea, hot coffee, or hot chocolate when it's cold outside? And in the summer, a nice glass of cold water or iced tea is refreshing. But lukewarm coffee or lukewarm tea isn't too desirable. In fact, if you were at a restaurant, you might even send it back.

Just as many people don't care for lukewarm drinks, Jesus doesn't care for lukewarm Christianity. He wants you either hot or cold for His kingdom. Half-hearted service and half-hearted devotion is worse than no service or devotion at all. It's placating the Savior who sacrificed His life for the forgiveness of sins. Jesus doesn't take too well to condescension or placating. In fact, He said it made Him want to vomit this church out of His mouth. That's a pretty harsh thing to say about someone. But He meant it, because even though they called themselves believers, Jesus could not use this church for His kingdom because they were spiritually powerless.

By calling this church to live hot, He was asking them to become full-time saints. He didn't want them to just worship Him on Sundays and then go back to the world's ways on Mondays. He wanted a whole-week, or whole-life, commitment to Him. Part-time Christianity does no one any good. That's why Jesus reminded them that their identity was to be in Him, not in their worldly gains. Secular success, power, or fame is not to define whether a person is spiritually successful. When someone thinks what they have, whom they know, or what they have achieved defines them, they're mistaken. Our identity is in our Creator, the maker of heaven and earth.

Jesus called this church to a greater level of commitment, because without commitment, you can't overcome Satan's strategies against you. Without spiritual commitment, there is no reality to a person's association with Jesus Christ. It's in name only. There's just religiosity. Spiritual verbosity is not intimate connectivity. That's why our relationship to Jesus Christ must be personal. It's not about rules. It's not about lists. It's not about what we say, post, or take part in. Your ability to overcome the opposition Satan throws at you is strictly tied to the authenticity of your relationship with Jesus. Only in Him will you find what you need to live the victorious Christian life.

Excerpted from chapter 8, *Living as an Overcomer*

CONNECT

After praying together, respond to these suggestions or questions, remembering that sharing is part of connecting with others.

1. What would you say has been the greatest benefit or principle you've gleaned from this study?

2. Have you had the opportunity to share anything you've learned with someone outside of the church? If so, what was their response?

3. What have you started to apply to your life as a result of this study?

CAPTURE

Settle back and watch Tony's video teaching, taking in what he's been led to share for this session. The next section will help you unpack what you hear.

CONCENTRATE

The following questions, suggestions, and Scripture passages are designed to guide your discussion in response to Tony's teaching in the video.

1. Read Revelation 3:14-22. What stands out to you as some of the worst things this church was doing?

2. According to Luke 9:24 (our Commit to Memory verse), what do you gain for sacrificing your life (your wants, desires, ambitions, renown) for the Lord's glory and gain?

3. Is there time for the church in Laodicea to repent? If so, what will happen as a result of their repenting?

4. Tony used the illustration of President Bush acknowledging his presence in front of an entire crowd of people at an event. How would you feel and what thoughts would you have if Jesus Christ were to single you out from others and acknowledge your being especially close to Him?

5. Read Revelation 3:18: "I advise you to buy from Me gold refined by fire so that you may become rich, and white garments so that you may clothe yourself, and *that* the shame of your nakedness will not be revealed; and eye salve to anoint your eyes so that you may see."

   What three things are these church members encouraged to do?

   1.

   2.

   3.

   What do you think these three things represent spiritually?

   1.

   2.

   3.

6. Read Revelation 3:19: "Those whom I love, I reprove and discipline; therefore be zealous and repent." What does God do to those whom He loves?

CONVERGE

Explore how what you've learned in this session can converge with your daily life—in other words, how you can apply it. As you discuss the following, jot down personal notes and proposed action steps in the extra space provided.

1. Describe how our contemporary Christian culture may reflect the church in Laodicea.

2. What role does personal sacrifice and authenticity play in overcoming?

3. Read Revelation 3:21: "He who overcomes, I will grant to him to sit down with Me on My throne, as I also overcame and sat down with My Father on His throne." What does it mean to sit down and dine with Jesus in our everyday efforts at overcoming?

4. Have you ever brought secular success into the church and relied on it rather than on God? Share some approaches to balancing secular success and spiritual dependence.

5. How can you commit to becoming a more authentic believer?

CONCLUDE

To close the session, first worship the Lord together in any way meaningful to the group, such as singing a song. Then before a final prayer, share any prayer requests or praise for answered prayer.

CONTINUE

This last section is for you to use on your own over the next week, proceeding through the five opportunities for reflection as you wish—perhaps one per day. Before you work through the Scripture and questions, ask the Lord to open your ears to truly hear His truth and for His help in applying it in your life. Then record what He reveals to you in the extra space provided.

1. Read Matthew 19:21: "Jesus said to him, 'If you wish to be complete, go and sell your possessions and give to the poor, and you will have treasure in heaven; and come, follow Me.'"

   ### Reflect
   According to Matthew 19:21, what do you need to do if you wish to be complete?

   Describe the difference between treasure on earth and treasure in heaven.

   Does following Jesus involve sacrifice? In what ways?

2. Read Luke 18:28-30: "Peter said, 'Behold, we have left our own homes and followed You.' And He said to them, 'Truly I say to you, there is no one who has left house or wife or brothers or parents or children, for the sake of the kingdom of God, who will not receive many times as much at this time and in the age to come, eternal life.'"

Reflect

What does Jesus say about anything you've given up for Him?

Does this apply only to eternity? Or does it also refer to earthly success? How so?

In what ways are you giving God the opportunity to reward you on earth and in eternity?

3. Read Acts 2:44-45: "All those who had believed were together and had all things in common; and they began selling their property and possessions and were sharing them with all, as anyone might have need."

Reflect

Describe the church of Acts 2.

Is giving out of your excess the same as giving of your own possessions? Explain.

In what ways do you strive to meet the needs of those around you?

4. Read Luke 14:33: "So then, none of you can be My disciple who does not give up all his own possessions."

Reflect
What does Jesus mean in Luke 14:33?

What is your heart's viewpoint on your own possessions?

In what ways can you adjust your thoughts, mindsets, and choices to better reflect the spirit of self-sacrifice Christ calls His followers to pursue?

5. Review Luke 9:24: "Whoever wishes to save his life will lose it, but whoever loses his life for My sake, he is the one who will save it."

Reflect

What do you think it means to lose your life for Christ's sake?

Are you willing to lay down your personal ambitions and desires in order to surrender all to God? How will you do that? Try to be specific.

In what way can you increase your level of sacrifice for God?

Why is it important to have an eternal perspective when it comes to temporal sacrifice?

THE URBAN ALTERNATIVE

The Urban Alternative (TUA) equips, empowers, and unites Christians to impact individuals, families, churches, and communities through a thoroughly kingdom-agenda worldview. In teaching truth, we seek to transform lives.

The core cause of the problems we face in our personal lives, homes, churches, and societies is a spiritual one. Therefore, the only way to address that core cause is spiritually. We've tried a political, social, economic, and even a religious agenda, and now it's time for a kingdom agenda.

The kingdom agenda can be defined as the visible manifestation of the comprehensive rule of God over every area of life.

The unifying central theme throughout the Bible is the glory of God and the advancement of His kingdom. The conjoining thread from Genesis to Revelation—from beginning to end—is focused on one thing: God's glory through advancing God's kingdom.

When we do not recognize that theme, the Bible becomes for us a series of disconnected stories that are great for inspiration but seem to be unrelated in purpose and direction. Understanding the role of the kingdom in Scripture increases our understanding of the relevancy of this several-thousand-year-old text to our day-to-day living. That's because God's kingdom was not only then; it is now.

The absence of the kingdom's influence in our personal lives, family lives, churches, and communities has led to a deterioration in our world of immense proportions:

- People live segmented, compartmentalized lives because they lack God's kingdom worldview.

- Families disintegrate because they exist for their own satisfaction rather than for the kingdom.

- Churches are limited in the scope of their impact because they fail to comprehend that the goal of the church is not the church itself but the kingdom.

- Communities have nowhere to turn to find real solutions for real people who have real problems because the church has become divided, in-grown, and unable to transform the cultural and political landscape in any relevant way.

By optimizing the solutions of heaven, the kingdom agenda offers us a way to see and live life with a solid hope. When God is no longer the final and authoritative standard under which all else falls, order and hope have left with Him. But the reverse of that is true as well: as long as we have God, we have hope. If God is still in the picture, and as long as His agenda is still on the table, it's not over.

Even if relationships collapse, God will sustain us. Even if finances dwindle, God will keep us. Even if dreams die, God will revive us. As long as God and His rule are still the overarching standard in our lives, families, churches, and communities, there is always hope.

Our world needs the King's agenda. Our churches need the King's agenda. Our families need the King's agenda.

We've put together a three-part plan to direct us to heal the divisions and strive for unity as we move toward the goal of truly being one nation under God. This three-part plan calls us to assemble with others in unity, to address the issues that divide us, and to act together for social impact. Following this plan, we will see individuals, families, churches, and communities transformed as we follow God's kingdom agenda in every area of our lives. You can request this plan by texting the keyword "strategy" to 55659 or visiting TonyEvans.org/strategy.

In many major cities, drivers can take a loop to the other side of the city when they don't want to head straight through downtown. This loop takes them close enough to the city center so they can see its towering buildings and skyline but not close enough to actually experience it.

This is precisely what we, as a culture, have done with God. We have put Him on the "loop" of our personal, family, church, and community lives. He's close enough to be at hand should we need Him in an emergency but far enough away that He can't be the center of who we are. We want God on the "loop," not the King of the Bible who comes downtown into the very heart of our ways. And as we have seen in our own lives and in the lives of others, leaving God on the "loop" brings about dire consequences.

But when we make God, and His rule, the centerpiece of all we think, do, or say, we experience Him in the way He longs for us to experience Him. He wants us to be kingdom people with kingdom minds set on fulfilling His kingdom's purposes. He wants us to pray, as Jesus did, "Not My will, but Thy will be done" because His is the kingdom, the power, and the glory.

There is only one God, and we are not Him. As King and Creator, God calls the shots. Only when we align ourselves under His comprehensive hand will we access His full power and authority in all spheres of life: personal, familial, ecclesiastical, and governmental.

As we learn how to govern ourselves under God, we then transform the institutions of family, church, and society using a biblically based kingdom worldview.

Under Him, we touch heaven and change earth.

To achieve our goal, we use a variety of strategies, approaches, and resources for reaching and equipping as many people as possible.

BROADCAST MEDIA

Millions of individuals experience *The Alternative with Dr. Tony Evans*, a daily broadcast on nearly 2,000 radio outlets and in more than 130 countries. The broadcast can also be seen on several television networks including TBN and Fox Business and is available online at TonyEvans.org. You can also listen to or view the daily broadcast by downloading the Tony Evans app for free in the App Store. More than 60,000,000 message downloads/streams occur each year.

LEADERSHIP TRAINING

The *Tony Evans Training Center* (TETC) facilitates a comprehensive discipleship platform, which provides an educational program that embodies the ministry philosophy of Dr. Tony Evans as expressed through the kingdom agenda. The training courses focus on leadership development and discipleship in the following five tracks:

1. Bible and Theology

2. Individual Spiritual Growth

3. Family and Relationships

4. Church Health and Leadership Development

5. Society and Community Impact Strategies

The TETC program includes courses for both local and online students. Furthermore, TETC programming includes course work for nonstudent attendees. Pastors, Christian leaders, and Christian laity—both local and at a distance—can seek out the Kingdom Agenda Certificate for personal, spiritual, and professional development. For more information, visit TonyEvansTraining.org.

Kingdom Agenda Pastors (KAP) provides a viable network for like-minded pastors who embrace the kingdom agenda philosophy. Pastors have the opportunity to go deeper with Dr. Tony Evans as they are given greater biblical knowledge, practical applications, and resources to impact individuals, families, churches, and communities. KAP welcomes senior and associate pastors of all churches. KAP also offers an annual Summit held each year in Dallas with intensive seminars, workshops, and resources. For more information, visit KAFellowship.org.

Pastors' Wives Ministry, founded by the late Dr. Lois Evans, provides counsel, encouragement, and spiritual resources for pastors' wives as they serve with their husbands in the ministry. A primary focus of the ministry is the KAP Summit, where senior pastors' wives have a safe place to reflect, renew, and relax along with receiving training in personal development, spiritual growth, and care for their emotional and physical well-being. For more information, visit LoisEvans.org.

KINGDOM COMMUNITY IMPACT

The outreach programs of The Urban Alternative seek to provide positive impact on individuals, churches, families, and communities through a variety of ministries. We see these efforts as necessary to our calling as a ministry and essential to the communities we serve. With training on how to initiate and maintain programs to adopt schools, provide homeless services, and partner toward unity and justice with the local police precincts, which creates a connection between the police and our community, we, as a ministry, live out God's kingdom agenda according to our *Kingdom Strategy for Community Transformation.*

The *Kingdom Strategy for Community Transformation* is a three-part plan that equips churches to have a positive impact on their communities for the kingdom of God. It also provides numerous practical suggestions for how this three-part plan can be implemented in your community, and it serves as a blueprint for unifying churches around the common goal of creating a better world for all of us. For more information, visit TonyEvans.org, then click on the link to access the 3-Point Plan. A course for this strategy is also offered online through the Tony Evans Training Center.

Tony Evans Films ushers in positive life change through compelling video-shorts, animation, and feature-length films. We seek to build kingdom disciples through the power of story. We use a variety of platforms for viewer consumption and have 220,000,000+ digital views. We also merge video-shorts and film with relevant Bible study materials to bring people to the saving knowledge of Jesus Christ and to strengthen the body of Christ worldwide. Tony Evans Films released its first feature-length film, *Kingdom Men Rising*, in April 2019 in more than 800 theaters nationwide in partnership with Lifeway Films. The second release, *Journey with Jesus*, is in partnership with RightNow Media and was released for three nights of nearly 1,000 sold-out theaters in November 2021. The third release is *Unbound: The Bible's Journey Through History*, a documentary focusing on the transmission of the Bible from the third through the sixteenth centuries.

RESOURCE DEVELOPMENT

By providing a variety of published materials, we are fostering lifelong learning partnerships with the people we serve. Dr. Evans has published more than 125 unique titles based on more than 50 years of preaching—in booklet, book, or Bible study format. He also holds the honor of writing and publishing the first full-Bible commentary and study Bible by an African American, released in 2019. This Bible sits in permanent display as a historic release in the Museum of the Bible in Washington, DC.

For more information, and to opt-in to Dr. Evans' devotional email, text the word "DEVO" to 55659, call (800) 800-3222, or visit us online at:

www.TonyEvans.org/devo

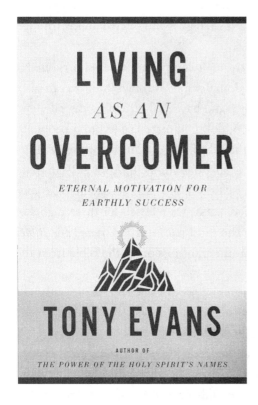

"He who has an ear, let him hear what the Spirit says to the churches."

REVELATION 2:7

The unique hardships of our modern lives can often feel insurmountable. But God's Word reveals to us that there is no obstacle, habit, or situation we face that Jesus hasn't already given us the power to conquer.

In *Living as an Overcomer*, bestselling author Dr. Tony Evans examines how Christ's message to the seven churches in Revelation can challenge, convict, and lead you toward emphatic victory over any difficulty in life. Through this powerful portion of Scripture, Dr. Evans helps you

- discover how Christ's words to some of the earliest churches brim with enduring life and relevance, even in our contemporary context

- rekindle your deepest convictions and strengthen your spiritual commitment as Christ's admonitions and promises permeate your heart

- vanquish obstacles and live triumphantly by laying claim to all God has in store for you

As you heed God's instructions to the early church, you will receive everything you need to experience victory over sin and prevail in your present circumstances. Reject lukewarm faith and start living as an overcomer!

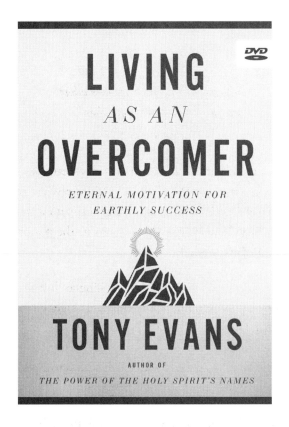

LIVING
AS AN
OVERCOMER

ETERNAL MOTIVATION FOR
EARTHLY SUCCESS

TONY EVANS

AUTHOR OF
THE POWER OF THE HOLY SPIRIT'S NAMES

Be Challenged to Live Triumphantly

Every believer can be assured that God has already given us everything we need to experience victory over sin. In the dynamic videos on the *Living as an Overcomer DVD*, Dr. Tony Evans helps you see how you can triumph over life's difficulties by taking heed of Christ's message to the seven churches in Revelation.

These sessions with Dr. Evans will also help you rekindle your deepest convictions and strengthen your spiritual commitment as Christ calls you to return to your first love with Him. Get ready to vanquish obstacles and prevail in your present circumstances by laying claim to all that your loving Father has in store for you.

While the unique hardships of our modern lives can often feel insurmountable, you will discover how Jesus' message to some of the earliest churches brims with power and relevance even in our contemporary context.

To learn more about Harvest House books and
to read sample chapters, visit our website:

www.HarvestHousePublishers.com

HARVEST HOUSE PUBLISHERS
EUGENE, OREGON